D0364625
3 0116 02019184 5

CHILDREN LIKE US

SCHOOLS

AROUND THE WORLD

Moira Butterfield

WAYLAND
www.waylandbooks.co.uk

First published in Great Britain in 2016
by Wayland

© Wayland, 2016

All rights reserved.

ISBN: 978 0 7502 9613 7

10 9 8 7 6 5 4 3 2 1

Wayland
An imprint of
Hachette Children's Group
Part of Hodder & Stoughton
Carmelite House
50 Victoria Embankment
London EC4Y 0DZ

An Hachette UK Company
www.hachette.co.uk
www.hachettechildrens.co.uk

Printed in China

Produced for Wayland by:
White-Thomson Publishing Ltd
www.wtpub.co.uk

Editor: Izzi Howell
Designer: Clare Nicholas
Picture researcher: Izzi Howell
Proofreaders: Izzi Howell/Stephen White-Thomson
Wayland editor: Annabel Stones

Picture credits:
The author and publisher would like to thank the following for allowing their pictures to be reproduced in this publication: cover (l-r, t-b) Bartosz Hadyniak/iStock, blackred/iStock, pyzata/iStock, skodonnell/iStock, Jerome Levitch/Corbis, rzoze19/Shutterstock, Richard Peterson/Shutterstock, Hugh Sitton/Corbis, RHIMAGE/Shutterstock, Bartosz Hadyniak/iStock; back cover (t/b) skodonnell/iStock, (l) pyzata/iStock, (r) Gail Palethorpe/Shutterstock; title page (l-r, t-b) Bartosz Hadyniak/iStock, blackred/iStock, pyzata/iStock, skodonnell/iStock, Gail Palethorpe/Shutterstock, rzoze19/Shutterstock, Richard Peterson/Shutterstock, Necip Yanmaz/iStock, RHIMAGE/Shutterstock, Bartosz Hadyniak/iStock; p.3 (t-b) Aleksandar Todorovic/Shutterstock, demerzel21/iStock, Gail Palethorpe/Shutterstock, Vikram Raghuvanshi/iStock; pp.4-5 (c) ekler/Shutterstock; p.4 (t) Christopher Futcher/iStock, (b) ajman33/iStock; p.5 (tl) Dominik Pabis/iStock, (tr) li jianbing/Shutterstock, (br) nguyenkhacthanh/Shutterstock; p.6 (t) DavorLovincic/iStock, (c) Dominik Pabis/iStock, (b) Frederic Soltan/Corbis; p.7 EdStock/iStock; p.8 epa/Corbis; p.9 (t) danishkhan/iStock, (b) Bill Bachman / Alamy; p.10 (t) demerzel21/iStock, (b) nguyenkhacthanh/Shutterstock; p.11 Hugh Sitton/Corbis; p.12 (tr) Grigvovan/Shutterstock, (bl) Aaron Huey/National Geographic Creative/Corbis, (br) egorovnick/Shutterstock; p.13 Radius Images/Corbis; p.14 (tl) BartCo/iStock, (cr) Hugh Sitton/Corbis, (bl) ajman33/iStock; p.15 Ton Koene/Visuals Unlimited/Corbis; p.16 (tr) Tomas van Houtryve/VII/Corbis, (bl) Vikram Raghuvanshi/iStock, (br) Bartosz Hadyniak/iStock; p.17 Thierry Tronnel/Corbis; p.18 (tl) xPACIFICA/Corbis, (cl) bruniewska/iStock, (br) Christopher Futcher/iStock; p.19 Sanjeev Gupta/epa/Corbis; p.20 (tr) pamspix/iStock, (cr) Karen Kasmauski/Corbis, (bl) Studio-Annika/iStock; p.21 Tuul & Bruno Morandi/Corbis; p.22 (t) Dougal Thomas/Corbis, (b) li jianbing/Shutterstock; p.23 Gideon Mendel/In Pictures/Corbis; p.24 Thomas Mukoya/Reuters/Corbis; p.25 (t) Gail Palethorpe/Shutterstock, Baciu/Shutterstock; p.26 (tr) Aaron Huey/National Geographic Creative/Corbis, (bl and br) Necip Yanmaz/iStock; p.27 Randy Olson/National Geographic Creative/Corbis; p.28 (tr) Fritz Hoffmann/In Pictures/Corbis, (bl) idome/Shutterstock, (br) Aleksandar Todorovic/Shutterstock; p.29 Krishnendu Halder/Reuters/Corbis; p.30 (l-r, t-b) idome/Shutterstock, bruniewska/iStock, Christopher Futcher/iStock, Necip Yanmaz/iStock, Studio-Annika/iStock, EdStock/iStock, li jianbing/Shutterstock, pamspix/iStock, Baciu/Shutterstock, danishkhan/iStock, BartCo/iStock, Grigvovan/Shutterstock, Bartosz Hadyniak/iStock; p.31 (l) ajman33/iStock, (r) nguyenkhacthanh/Shutterstock.

Design elements used throughout: Moofer/Shutterstock, rassco/Shutterstock, lilac/Shutterstock, gladcov/Shutterstock, Matthew Cole/Shutterstock, Dacian G/Shutterstock, Malchev/Shutterstock, sommthink/Shutterstock, Studio Barcelona/Shutterstock, katarina_1/Shutterstock, Popmarleo/Shutterstock, Divergenta/Shutterstock, Spreadthesign/Shutterstock, Juli Hansen/Shutterstock, VikaSuh/Shutterstock, Ingka D. Jiw/Shutterstock.

Every effort has been made to clear copyright. Should there be any inadvertent omission, please apply to the publisher for rectification.

The website addresses (URLs) included in this book were valid at the time of going to press. However, it is possible that contents or addresses may have changed since the publication of this book. No responsibility for any such changes can be accepted by either the author or the Publisher.

Contents

All Kinds of Schools 4
Off to School 6
Big Schools, Small Schools 8
Schools in Hot Places 10
Schools in Cold Places 12
School Clothes 14
How We Learn 16
School Sports 18
Performing at School 20
Break Time! 22
Lunch at School 24
Living at School 26
Surprising Schools 28
Art Station 30
Glossary 31
Further Reading 32
Index 32

All Kinds of Schools

Are you ready to travel around the world and find out about the school days of children just like you? You'll travel to schools in busy cities and tiny villages, discover different kinds of classrooms and school clothes, and learn about children who live at school.

School sports are different around the world. Find out about the para-sport that these American children are doing on page 18.

There are many types of school uniform. Find out about this Peruvian boy's woollen school hat on page 14.

Children play their favourite games at break time. Find out about the game that these Chinese girls are playing on page 22.

Children travel to school on different kinds of transport. Discover how these Indian schoolgirls get to class on page 6.

Classrooms are different all over the world. Can you guess why these Vietnamese schoolchildren have lessons outside? Find out why on page 10.

Take a journey around the world to discover the schools of children just like you!

Off to School

In Asian countries, children in cities often travel to school by rickshaw or tuk-tuk. These small vehicles can squeeze through the busy city streets without getting stuck in traffic. No one wants to be late for school, so rickshaws and tuk-tuks are often piled high with children in the mornings and afternoons.

A rickshaw is a three-wheeled bicycle taxi with the driver pedalling at the front.

A tuk-tuk is a three-wheeled motorbike taxi with a roof to shelter the passengers.

For city children, taking the subway to school is often quicker than driving through the crowded streets in the city above. These schoolchildren are making their journey by subway in Tokyo, Japan.

These Japanese children are carrying their school books in a backpack called a randoseru.

The children of Gulucun live high up above a steep canyon in a mountainous region of China. To get to school, they walk along a narrow mountain path, high above the canyon. Some of the children walk for three hours to get to school.

These Chinese children walk to school along a 1500 metre-high path.

Big Schools, Small Schools

The world's biggest school is the City Montessori School in the city of Lucknow in India. When the school first started, it had five pupils. Today, the school has 47,000 pupils and 3,800 members of staff! As there are so many pupils, the school's 1,000 classrooms are spread across the city.

On Children's Day in India, all the pupils and teachers at the world's largest school get together to celebrate. The crowd is big enough to fill a football stadium!

The Street School in Lyari, Pakistan is so small that it doesn't even have a building. Instead, it's run in a curtained-off corner of a busy street. When the school first opened, it was hidden from the street by a curtain made from old flour bags, and the children sat on mats on the floor. Now the school has more equipment, thanks to charity donations.

These tiny classes are part of the Street School, which was set up in 1985 to teach poor children in this busy city street in Pakistan.

Australian School of the Air students speak to their teachers using video cameras and microphones.

This Australian girl is the only pupil in her class! She's studying long-distance with the School of the Air, because she lives a long way from the nearest school. School of the Air teachers use technology to give online classes to students living in different areas of the Australian outback.

Schools in Hot Places

In tropical climates, it can be very warm and sometimes very rainy. This outdoor classroom in eastern Ghana has a roof to keep the rain out, but no walls, so there is plenty of cooling air. The children can see the rainforest from their school desks.

The weather can get hot and steamy in Ghana, but this classroom has its own natural air conditioning.

This classroom is completely outdoors. In Yen Bai, a mountainous part of Vietnam, class is held outside in summer when it's warm. The children go back inside the school in winter when it's rainy and cold.

The children at this Vietnamese school move their desks and benches outside in summer.

These children live in a village in the Amazon rainforest in Ecuador, South America. Their school building is an open-sided grass hut with an earth floor. It was built using dried plants from the rainforest that surrounds the village. In the background, you can see one of the houses where the village people live.

These Ecuadorian children learn in a classroom with a roof made of dried grasses, and they wear dried grass skirts, too.

OC SINH TÍCH CỰC!

Schools in Cold Places

Does your school have central heating for when it's cold? If you went to this school in Tver, Russia, you would have a wood-burning fireplace to keep you warm instead. Winters are snowy and cold in Tver, so the fire is kept burning through the school day.

This Russian schoolgirl has found a warm spot near the classroom fireplace.

Ushguli is the highest community in Europe, nestled among high, snowy mountains in Georgia. These children are playing inside during a winter break time because it's cold and snowy outdoors. In winter, their remote village can sometimes be cut off from the outside world by heavy snow.

These Georgian schoolchildren keep their coats and hats on in school because it is so cold in winter.

The villages in Ushguli are covered in snow for six months of the year.

These Norwegian children are learning how to ski with their teacher.

In winter, all schools in Norway have a regular Ski Day. Instead of indoor lessons, everybody goes outside to learn skiing for the day. Norwegian children often learn to ski from around the age of three. It's no wonder that Norway has won so many Winter Olympics sports medals!

School Clothes

The children in this Malaysian school are Muslims. For religious reasons, the girls cover their heads with a long headscarf called a tudung. The girls wear long-sleeved tunics and skirts called baju kurung, and the boys wear caps called songkok.

These school uniforms are based on traditional clothing worn by Malaysian Muslims.

In the high Andes Mountains in South America, Quechua children wear warm clothes to school. This girl is wearing a jobona – a woollen jacket decorated with ribbons – and a traditional montera hat.

To keep warm at break time, this boy from the Peruvian island of Taquile is wearing a woollen hat that he knitted himself.

This Peruvian Quechua girl is wearing a warm jobona jacket made from llama or alpaca wool.

The Xingu people often use tiny sticks and dyes made from rainforest plants to draw patterns on their faces.

This boy is sitting in a village school near the Xingu River in the Brazilian Amazon. At his school, they don't wear uniforms – they are allowed to wear their everyday clothing in class. He is dressed for the heat with a cloth tied round his legs and waist and no shirt. His headdress is made from parrot feathers.

How We Learn

In some schools, children use technology to learn in an interactive way. Instead of blackboards, teachers can use electronic whiteboards to show their students websites and videos. Students can write using laptops or tablets instead of pens and paper.

In this South Korean school, a robot puppy is programmed to play educational games with the children. The puppy responds to touch, sound and movement.

These children are learning in a village school in Ratnagiri, a rural part of India. Their classroom doesn't have chairs or desks – the children sit on soft rugs on the floor. Their teacher is using chalk to write on a blackboard. He can clean the writing off the blackboard with a cloth when he wants to write something new.

These Indian schoolchildren learn by reading from a blackboard.

This Ethiopian girl has been asked by her teacher to write on the blackboard.

These Chinese children come from a poor community where people do not have the money for modern equipment.

These boys are carrying their abacuses to school in Baisha-Yunnan, China. The wooden abacuses slung around their necks are fitted with beads to help them do maths. They belong to the Nakhi community who live in the foothills of the Himalayas, far away from modern schools with computers.

School Sports

Children at the Shaolin Tagou School in China start every day with martial arts exercises.

The children on the top left attend a school that specialises in sport. They go to the Shaolin Tagou Martial Arts School in Dengfeng, China. Over 13,000 pupils between the ages of six and 25 learn martial arts here every day, as well as studying ordinary subjects. It is the biggest martial arts school in the world.

The school day at this Indian school begins with yoga exercises in the playground.

These American children are practising wheelchair racing at their school. They have specially-designed sports wheelchairs, with lightweight frames and sloping wheels that help them to pick up extra speed.

Wheelchair racing is one of many para-sports for people with disabilities.

These schoolboys are taking part in an unusual and ancient sport at a school event in Bhopal, India. It's called mallakhamb, and it's a type of gymnastics performed with a long wooden pole or a rope. Mallakhamb interschool competitions are held in some regions of India.

The name mallakhamb comes from the word 'malla' which means 'athlete' and 'khamba' which means 'pole'.

Performing at School

This Australian school drumming band is taking part in an Anzac Day parade.

Drumming is a popular type of music all over the world and it's taught in many schools. Some schools even have their own drumming bands that perform at school events. These Tanzanian girls are performing at an event to celebrate Tanzania's Independence Day.

These girls have drums painted in the colours of Tanzania's flag.

These schoolchildren are dressed as the Three Kings, arriving to give presents to the baby Jesus.

In some Christian countries, Christmas nativity plays are traditional in primary schools. The word 'nativity' means birth, and a nativity play follows the Bible story of Jesus's birth in a stable. Live stable animals, such as donkeys and sheep, sometimes take part in the play, or children dress in animal costumes.

Schoolchildren often learn dances that are traditional in their country. These Cambodian schoolgirls have learnt an ancient type of Cambodian dance called Aspara. They are using graceful body movements to represent characters from Cambodian legends.

Aspara is a type of Cambodian dance. In other countries, children will learn their own local dances at school.

Break Time!

These schoolchildren are playing football at break time at a school near Nairobi, Kenya.

Ball games, especially football, are popular at break time all over the world. Football is said to be played by 256 million men and women worldwide, and that's just official recorded matches. Children set up football games for themselves in playgrounds all over the planet.

Children are shown skipping in paintings from around 600 years ago, so we know that skipping has been a popular game for many centuries. Skipping ropes are still used in playgrounds all over the world because they are a great way to play alone or together.

This Chinese girl is bending her knees to help her jump high above the skipping rope.

Tig, Tap and Dobby are all British names for the playground game of tag. It has many different names around the world.

These British primary schoolchildren are playing a break-time game of tag. There are many versions of tag in different countries, but they all involve one important rule – 'If you're caught, you're IT!'.

Lunch at School

Without his porridge at school, this Somali boy might not get enough food to stay healthy.

This Somali boy has been given a bowl of porridge at lunchtime. He goes to school in a refugee camp in Kenya, because he lost his home when war broke out in his country. His school dinner is very important for him because there isn't much food in the refugee camp.

Many children bring a packed lunch to school. These Burmese children carry their packed lunch in round, metal containers called tiffin boxes. The tiffin boxes are stacked together, each box carrying something different – a piece of bread, some rice, or a spicy meat or vegetable stew.

Metal tiffin boxes are used for packed lunches all over Asia.

At this Indian school, older students serve school dinners to the younger students.

Some schools serve hot school dinners, prepared and cooked in the school kitchen. Today, these Indian schoolchildren from the city of Ladakh might be having skir (vegetable or meat stew) with moe moe (dumplings) and perhaps a piece of khambir (bread).

Living at School

At boarding school, children live at school, going home at weekends or during the school holidays. These students at a Nepalese boarding school are the children of Sherpa climbers. There aren't many schools in the high mountains where the Sherpa people live, so Sherpa children are often sent to boarding school.

In this Nepalese boarding school, they are celebrating somebody's birthday with a classroom banner.

These girls live and study at the Kayaywa Tawya Buddhist monastery in Burma. Here, they learn to be Buddhist nuns as well as having ordinary lessons. Most of them are orphans with no family, so their school is also their full-time home. Without the monastery, it is likely they would have no home or education.

These girls learn the teachings of Buddha as well as doing ordinary lessons.

It's easy to find classmates to help you with your homework when you live at a Buddhist monastery.

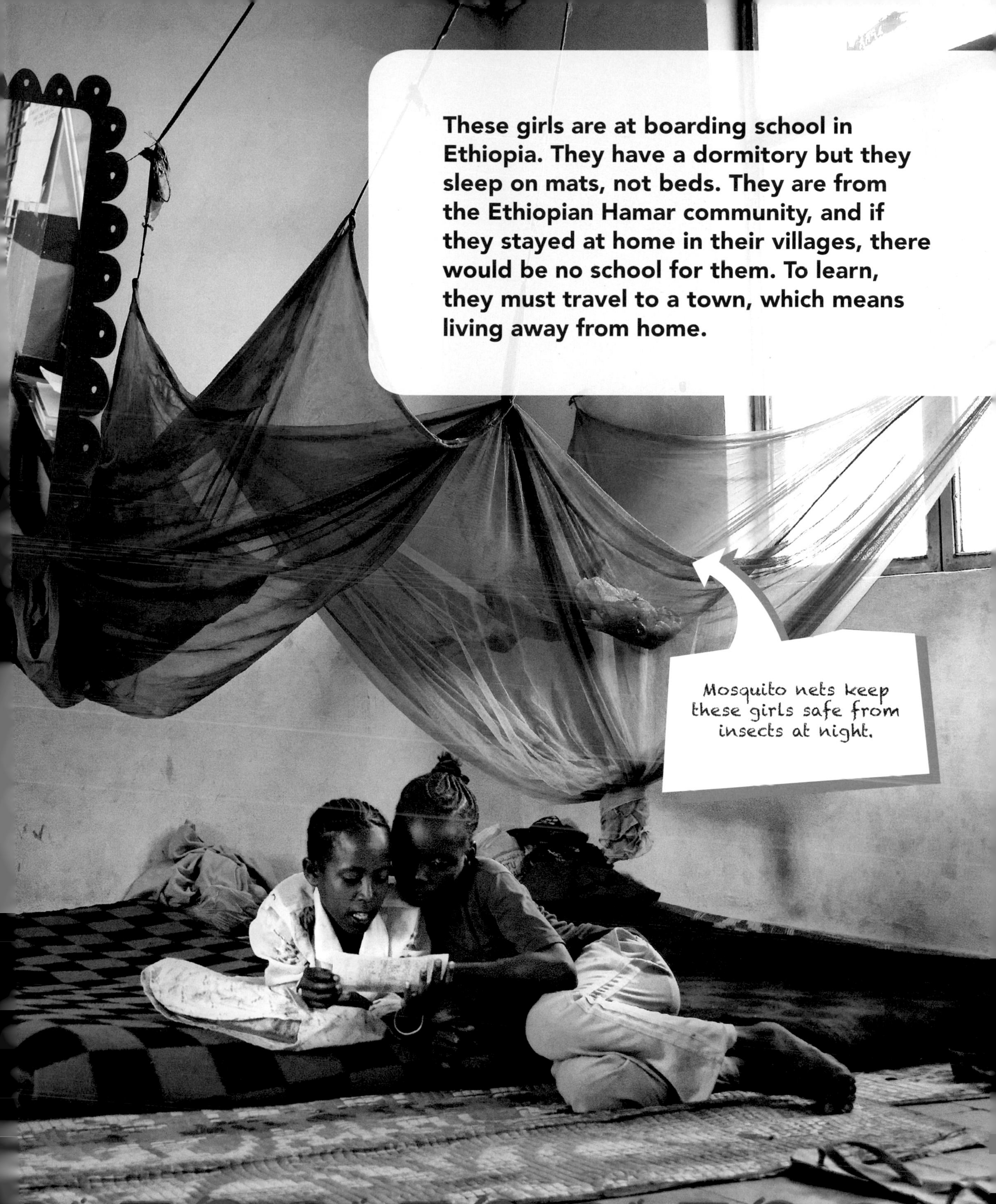

These girls are at boarding school in Ethiopia. They have a dormitory but they sleep on mats, not beds. They are from the Ethiopian Hamar community, and if they stayed at home in their villages, there would be no school for them. To learn, they must travel to a town, which means living away from home.

Mosquito nets keep these girls safe from insects at night.

Surprising Schools

There isn't room for many students in this Chinese cave classroom.

These Chinese children have a very unusual school. It's in a cave room cut into a hillside in the region where they live in Shaanxi, China. Many people live in cave homes in this area of China.

Children who come from local fishing families go to this school on a lake in Cambodia.

The school is the blue building on the left. The red building is the village police station.

Children go to school by rowing boat on the Tonlé Sap lake in Cambodia. They live in a floating village on the lake, in homes on stilts. Their school is high above the water, and they climb up to it from their boats.

The School on Wheels is a school on a bus that parks in different areas of Hyderabad, India. It is run for children from poor families. Without the School on Wheels, they probably wouldn't go to school at all, either because there is no school building where they live or because their families want them to work instead.

The School on Wheels encourages children from poor areas of India to learn reading, writing and maths for a few hours each week.

Art Station

Here are some ideas to help you get creative, and think about schools at the same time.

- **Design a new building for your school. Label which lessons will be taught inside your new building.**
- **Invent a new school and draw it. Give it a name and an address. Make up the name of a head teacher, too.**
- **Design a school uniform. Label it and colour it in.**
- **Take some photos around your school. Print them and cut them out. Then stick some of the pictures on a new piece of paper to make a collage that represents your school.**

Glossary

abacus a row of beads used for counting

air conditioning a system for sending cool air round a building

Buddhist someone who believes in the teachings of Buddha

central heating a heating system in a building

Christian people who believe in the teachings of Jesus

community a group of people living in one area

donation money or items given for free

dormitory a bedroom for several people at a boarding school

Muslim people who believe in the religion of Islam

para-sport sport designed for people with disabilities

refugee someone who has lost their home and had to leave their country

remote far away from anywhere

rural in the countryside

subway an underground railway under a city

traditional something that has happened for a long time

tropical an area around the middle of the world which is warm and rainy

Further Information

Websites

Information about school lunches around the world.
http://news.bbc.co.uk/cbbcnews/hi/newsid_4300000/newsid_4308600/4308635.stm

Some classrooms around the world.
http://www.theguardian.com/education/gallery/2012/sep/14/schools-around-the-world-children

Pictures of children going to school around the world.
http://www.travelchannel.com/interests/family/photos/back-to-school-around-the-world

Further Reading

Discover Countries series
(Wayland, 2015)

Mapping A Country series
Jen Green (Wayland, 2015)

Your Local Area: Schools
Ruth Thomson (Wayland, 2013)

Index

boarding schools 26–27

cities 4, 6, 8, 9, 25, 29
classrooms 4, 5, 8, 9, 10, 11, 12, 16, 26, 28, 29
computers 17

dance 21
dinners, school 25

food 24–25

games 5, 12, 16, 22–23

laptops 16

maths 17, 29
music 20

packed lunches 25
playgrounds 18, 22, 23
plays 20

religions 14, 26

School of the Air, Australian 9
School on Wheels 29
sports 13, 18–19, 22

teachers 8, 9, 13, 16
technology 9, 16, 17
transport 4, 5, 6–7

uniforms 4, 11, 12, 14–15

villages 4, 11, 12, 15, 16, 27, 28

CHILDREN LIKE US

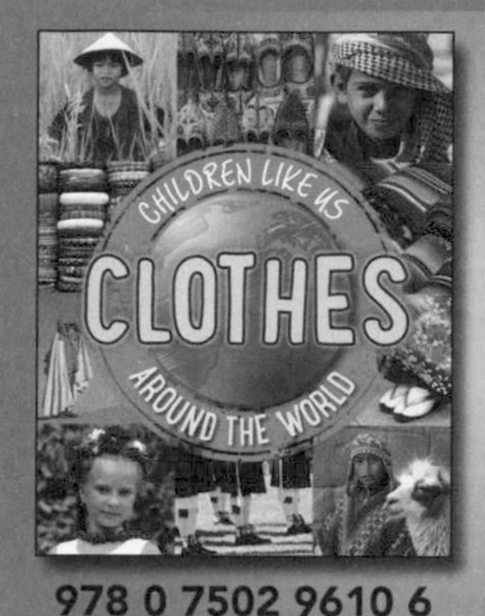

All Kinds of Clothes
Dress for a Festival
National Costume
Clothes in the Snow
Clothes in the Sun
Clothes in the Rainforest
Dress for Dancing
Colourful Clothes
Working Clothes
Clothes for Special Days
Special Shoes
Fantastic Hats
All Kinds of Jewellery
Art Station

978 0 7502 9610 6

All Kinds of Food
What's for Breakfast?
What's for Lunch?
What's for Dinner?
Festival Food
Wedding Food
Sweet Treats
Delicious Drinks
Fantastic Fruit
All Kinds of Vegetables
Scrummy Bread
Street Eating
Now THAT'S Different!
Art Station

978 0 7502 9612 0

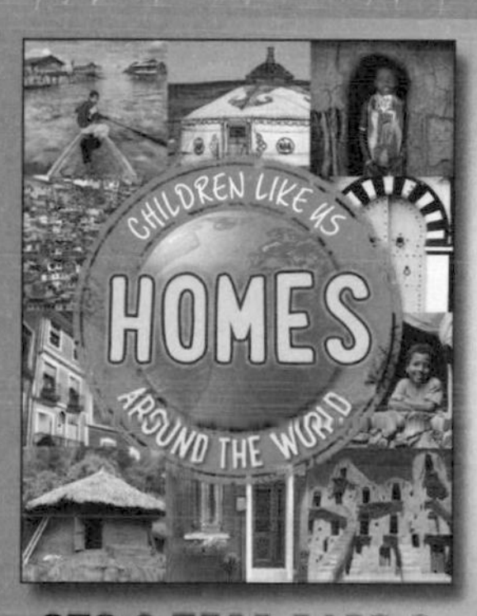

All Kinds of Homes
Homes on the Water
Homes in the City
A Tent Home
A Thatched Home
A Home on Wheels
Communal Homes
A Home in the Snow
A Home in the Mountains
Green Homes
An Underground Home
Decorated Homes
Unusual Homes
Art Station

978 0 7502 9609 0

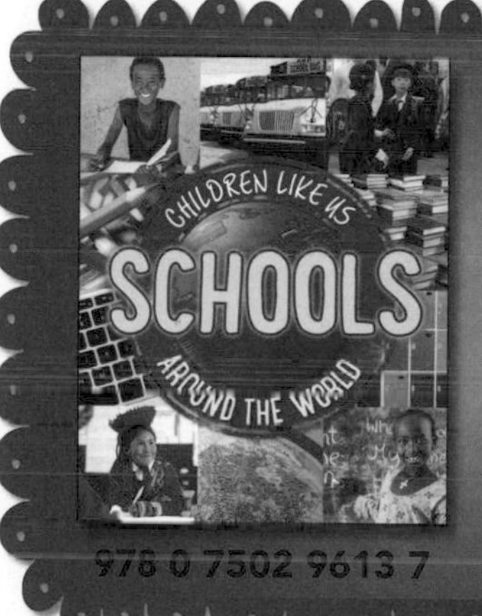

All Kinds of Schools
Off to School
Big Schools, Small Schools
Schools in Hot Places
Schools in Cold Places
School Clothes
How We Learn
School Sports
Performing at School
Break Time!
Lunch at School
Living at School
Surprising Schools
Art Station

978 0 7502 9613 7

All Kinds of Toys and Games
City Games
Countryside Playtime
Fun in the Snow
Wonderful Water Toys
Brilliant Board Games
Making Music
Electronic Fun
Homemade Toys
All Sorts of Dolls
Super Sports
All Sorts of Wheels
Flying Toys
Art Station

978 0 7502 9614 4

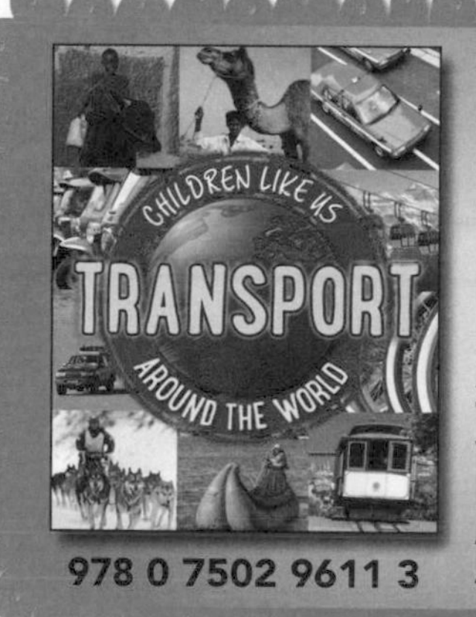

All Kinds of Transport
Cross a City
Ride on Water
Through the Snow
Take to the Tracks
Explore a Desert
Up the Mountain
Festival Transport
All Kinds of Horses
Take to the Air
Win a Race
Decorated Transport
Amazing Transport
Art Station

978 0 7502 9611 3

WAYLAND
www.waylandbooks.co.uk